Sundays and Hot Buttered Rolls:

A Granddaughter of Harlem Speaks

poems by

Carla M. Cherry

Finishing Line Press
Georgetown, Kentucky

Sundays and Hot Buttered Rolls:

A Granddaughter of Harlem Speaks

Copyright © 2024 by Carla M. Cherry
ISBN 979-8-88838-567-8 First Edition
All rights reserved under International and Pan-American Copyright Conventions. No part of this book may be reproduced in any manner whatsoever without written permission from the publisher, except in the case of brief quotations embodied in critical articles and reviews.

ACKNOWLEDGMENTS

"Ode to Harlem" won first prize in Art Crawl Harlem's Fire and Soul: 100 Years of Harlem poetry competition in December 2020. It was published on Art Crawl Harlem's website and in Issue 7 of *Beliveau Review* in the Spring 2021.

"We've Been Dancing Since We Heard Our Mothers' Heartbeats In The Womb" and "Counterstroke" were first published in Volume 7, Issue 1 of *Rigorous*.

Publisher: Leah Huete de Maines
Editor: Christen Kincaid
Cover Art: AZS Art Studio
Author Photo: Amparo Peterkin
Cover Design: Elizabeth Maines McCleavy

Order online: www.finishinglinepress.com
also available on amazon.com

Author inquiries and mail orders:
Finishing Line Press
PO Box 1626
Georgetown, Kentucky 40324
USA

Contents

Ode to Harlem 1

An Afternoon at the Schomburg 6

A Day in the Studio 8

Grief 10

Sold 12

We've Been Dancing Since We Heard Our Mothers' Heartbeats

    in The Womb 14

Counterstroke 20

*For my father,
Melvin L. Cherry*

Ode to Harlem

I met Harlem through my father's eyes.
Daddy, a son of 375 Edgecombe Avenue.

Harlem.
A place that fed you, mind, body, and soul,
if you were in a good building with good neighbors.
P.S. 46.
Stitt Junior High School 164.
George Washington High School.
Daddy's favorite teacher, Mrs. Purcell, had parties
every Friday if the class was good.
Her voice, woo, was like a thunderclap.

You had your street gangs,
like the Egyptian Kings or the Debs,
but if your parents kept a tight rein on you,
you were OK,
and Nana and Pop-Pop
kept Daddy close to the stoop.

After school, there were
Boy Scouts, Cub Scouts, Explorers,
Brownies, Girl Scouts.
Minisink Townhouse.

Got around on streetcars on Amsterdam Avenue.
Double-decker buses on Broadway.
They cost ten, fifteen cents.
Ran from the Cloisters,
down Fifth Avenue.

Daddy sang
in the boys' choir at St. Luke's Episcopalian.
Baptized at Abyssinian Baptist Church.

Age 11, he carried groceries
at Food Family Supermarket
on 148th and St. Nicholas,
next door to the liquor store
David Dinkins' father-in-law used to own.

Daddy wandered the shelves of
Michaux's African National Memorial,
and Black Liberation Bookstore.

His friend Bunky
OD'd at the age of 16.
Daddy swore heroin
was dumped in Harlem
in the fifties
because of Adam Clayton Powell
and black people
starting to control their own destiny.
Destroy the youth,
destroy the community.

I met Harlem
through my father's eyes.
We read *The Amsterdam News*.
Four years of Saturdays
at Harlem School of the Arts—
piano and flute for me,
piano and ballet for my sister.
Black Liberation Bookstore after.
Read to Ms. Mulzac in polysyllabic breeze.
On to Better Pie Crust,
when we begged for cinnamon buns.
No sticky fingers on book covers.

Took us to the Schomburg
when he researched our family's roots,
buried deep in North Carolina's
peanut and cotton fields.

He bought a copy of *Harlem on My Mind*.
To see Harlem through my father's eyes,
I pored over its photos and articles
until the spine splintered:
>James Van Der Zee
>Speakeasies
>Ethel Waters
>Florence Mills
>Kid Chocolate
>Marcus Garvey and his Black Star Line
>Father Divine
>Joe Louis
>Rent strikes
>Protests
>boycotts—Don't buy here. Pass Them By.
>James Baldwin
>Percy Sutton
>Castro's visit at the Theresa Hotel.
>James Powell and the riots of '64.
>Malcolm X on the podium, then lying in state.

Family dinners
at 22 West on West 135th.
Copeland's where I ordered
entrees plus three sides.
As loved ones joined the Village of the Ancestors,
we held services at Benta's Funeral Home.

College summer breaks, I returned to Harlem.

Saw it through Daddy's eyes.
Went to Harlem Week.
Bought cassettes from The Record Shack.
Shopped for African garb at Mart 125.
Medallions, bracelets and
codfish cakes from the street vendors.

Like my father and mother,
I was baptized at Abyssinian.
I too strolled Strivers' Row on Sundays.
People said, Good Morning.
"Buy property," Reverend Butts said,
"I'm telling you now."

After service, coconut and vanilla cakes
from the cake and pie man
on the corner of West 138th
and Adam Clayton Powell Boulevard.
As music blasted from elders
selling gospel CDs,
we perused framed art that I would hang if I ever
owned a Harlem brownstone.

Though Mart 125,
The Record Shack, closed their doors,
rents went up,
big box stores took over,
new White neighbors called police
about loud music/laughter/domino games,
and not even the perfume
of the linden and sweet gum trees
could stop complaints
about the drum circle in Marcus Garvey Park
that kept it safer over 40 years,
this granddaughter of Harlem
is here to tell you
Harlem still feeds
the mind, body, and soul—
the churches where tourists
line up to hear Ze Gospel Music,

City College
the Schomburg
The Apollo
Studio Museum of Harlem
Sister's Uptown Bookstore
the people who say Good Morning on Strivers' Row,
Londel's
Ponty Bistro
Make My Cake
Melba's
The Cecil Steakhouse
Uptown Juice Bar.
Here I stand.

An Afternoon at the Schomburg

Dear Daddy,

I wish you could see me now,
in the Photographs and Prints Division.
Three boxes of original photos
from James Van Der Zee,
laid out before me,
and I get to look through them
one at a time.

I cannot make photocopies.
I must write the serial number
down for each picture I take
with my cell phone.
Flash off.

Wearing white cotton gloves,
I gently lift
each plastic-covered photograph.

So many I want to keep.
Marcus Garvey and his entourage.
J.A. Rogers, 1928.

I am trying to commit
each image to memory,

like the one that has become
my favorite—
a beautiful brown-skinned girl
in a white dress.

Even if it was
bedecked with pearls,
no aureate picture frame
could surround her face
as well as her curls.

She is seated,
her left leg over her right,
head tilted.

With the lodestone
of her smile,
she knew that
without her,
life in this realm
would be Earth
without an axis:

>	No golden cascade of leaves.
>	No snowfalls and silence.
>	No blooming of spring.
>	No summer sun and breezes.

A Day in the Studio

Dear Daddy,

It would have been
something
if Mr. Van Der Zee
had taken
the wedding portrait
when Nana and Pop-Pop
got married in '31.

Had they never heard of
The Picture Takin' Man?
Or was the sitting fee
too dear?

What kind of background
do you think Van Der Zee
would have painted?

A fireplace?
Candle?

Two smiling children
cross-legged on the floor?

How do you think
they would have posed?

Standing side by side?
Nana in a chair,
one hand neatly
over the other,
and Pop-Pop
standing beside
or behind her, smiling?

Or would Van Der Zee
have them sit next to each other,
gaze into each other's eyes
with connubial longing?

Twelve years
to have you,
then Aunt Joan
two years later.

Was a portrait of you four
on their wish list,
or
were they too busily grateful
for steady work
through the Depression
and World War II,
Pop-Pop at the Post Office,
Nana, and her day work,
money, devoted to
their clean and safe
two-bedroom on St. Nicholas Ave.
Tithes and offerings at Abyssinian.
Their car,
and summer drives down
to North Carolina.
Presents for your birthdays
and Christmases.
Sunday dinners
with Nana's homemade rolls with butter.

Grief

Dear Daddy,

I just discovered
James Van Der Zee's son Emil
died from pneumonia as a baby,
and he lost his daughter Rachel
when she was nineteen.
A ruptured appendix.

He photographed Rachel in her casket.
Her smiling,
superimposed face,
hovers above it.

You did not cry
in front of us
when we lost Nana,
then Pop-Pop.
When you spoke
at Aunt Joan's funeral
your voice only wavered once.

But I am sure
watching Donna,
your youngest,
the daughter
who looked most like you,
with tumors in her leg,
lungs, eyes,
the globe of one
sitting on her chest,

her crying out,
then passing away
before our eyes,

would have cracked
the left ventricle
of your heart
like the swing of a baseball bat.

If I could talk
to Mr. Van Der Zee
I would ask,

with Rachel
laid out before you,
how did you keep
your hands,
your eyes,
so steady?

Sold

Dear Daddy,

Thousands of people
streaming through the Met,
Van Der Zee's photos
the bulk of the exhibit,

and Van Der Zee and his wife
got evicted from their home
the day after
"Harlem on My Mind" closed.

Had you seen the article,
its pictures of
the Van Der Zees,
their possessions,
the boxes and bags
of 75,000 photos
on the street
in *The New York Times*?

Where were the protestors then?

Who could blame Gaynella
for spraying a city marshall
with a can of insect spray?

They restrained her
by tying her to a chair.

How could the woman
who bought their house
ignore the tears
in James's eyes
as he told the story
of the unpaid mortgage?

I can only hope
that revenants
haunted her dreams.

After they stuffed themselves
into that tiny apartment
on West 94th,
who knows how many times
James heard Gaynella demand,
Take me home.

How I wish Gaynella
had lived to see him
take portraits of
Eubie Blake
Cicely Tyson
Bill Cosby and his cigar
Ossie Davis and Ruby Dee
Jean-Michel Basquiat,
and receive
his Honorary Doctor of Letters
at Howard University.

I wonder if she,
Emil,
Rachel,
were there to take his hand
after Van Der Zee took his last breath.

The outline of the GGG Studio sign
still rests above
272 Lenox Avenue.

When folk walk that block of Lenox,
may they never fail
to look up.
Salute.

We've Been Dancing Since We Heard Our Mothers' Heartbeats in The Womb

Here we are.
Londel's. Frederick Douglass Boulevard.
Greeting each other
with perfumed hugs,
kisses on the cheek,
how-are-yous
complementing/complimenting
African glory.
High fashion.

Men in single-color
or African print shirts,
pressed slacks or denim jeans.
We ladies showing
just a smidgen of skin–
shoulders,
the diamond of our backs.

Sitting at tables,
menus in hand,
ordering collard greens,
potato salad,
fish and chips,
red velvet cake.

Swaying to Maze,
Stevie Wonder,
Felony Davis,
Marcell and the Truth.

Baby powder
in a couple of corners,
so when
our men come to us
with extended hands,
lead us to the center,

our strappy heels,
sandals, and canvas sneakers
can glide.

Willie Hutch's
"I Can Sho' Give You Love"
brings everybody to the floor.
Dresses and skirts,
blouses be blazing,
swinging.

Ceiling lights as spotlights,
sassy shine of
cocoa butter-softened ebon skin.
The black, brown,
and silver of our locs,
braids, twists,
teeny afros, afro puffs,
and curls glimmering.
We are doing it.

L.C. Henderson's eight-count step.
The basic.
Half-turns,
full right,
full left,
double turns,
box right,
box left.
Kickstand, Ticman,
backpedal, butterfly.
Extended-right, pitty-pat.
Side step, Strickland,
Suzy Q, shuffle.

We are here.
Like Langston, Countee, Zora,
and their pens.

We Sons and daughters
of Virginia, the Carolinas,
Georgia, Kentucky, Mississippi,
Alabama, Jamaica, Barbados.
Lawyers, teachers,
transit workers, social workers,
mothers, fathers, homeowners.
The many-great grandsons,
granddaughters,
sons and daughters of the
West African Circle Dance
ring shout
Juba
Cake Walk
Jitterbug
the bop
doing what our ancestors
have always done
since the ships
came in and out of New York Harbor
with sugar, tobacco, indigo, coffee,
chocolate, cotton,
enslaved Africans.
We know.

Slave-owning New Yorkers
only had one or two slaves,
but 41 percent
of New York City households had them.
They slept in cellars and attics,
above farmhouse kitchens
after long days of
bringing in the firewood,
the water,
cooking the food,
cleaning the houses
and the clothes.
Built Fort Amsterdam,

buildings along the Battery,
the wall around Wall Street,
roads, docks, the first City Hall,
first Dutch and English churches,
Fraunces Tavern,
the city prison and city hospital.

Prohibited from owning
or passing on property,
gathering in groups of more
than three, or at night,
from venturing north
of Worth Street.
Public punishment
for conspiracy to revolt.

The 419
at the African Burial Ground.
Our bodies riddled
with arthritis and rickets,
buried in coffins
decorated with a heart made of nails,
our heads facing West.
If we were lucky.

We know.

The Fugitive Slave Act.
The Draft Riots of 1863,
how white dockworkers
attacked and destroyed
tenements, dance halls, boarding houses,
brothels that catered to Blacks,
beat abolitionists
and burned down their homes.

As 233 Black orphans
were studying, playing,
resting in sick beds,

a crazed white mob
of adults and children
armed with clubs,
bricks, bats,
stole their bedding,
clothing, food, and
set their home on fire.
The orphans barely made it
out the back door.

We know how they hanged
William Jones and burned his body.
How they beat and almost drowned
Charles Jackson,
beat Jeremiah Robinson to death
and threw his body in the river.

How they jumped
on William Williams's chest,
stabbed him,
smashed his body with stones
while a crowd watched.
Pledged "vengeance on every nigger in New York."
How white laborer
George Glass dragged
black coachman Abraham Franklin
from his apartment,
and the mob
dragged him through the streets,
hanged him from a lamppost
as they cheered
for Jefferson Davis,
pulled Franklin's body
from the lamppost,
and sixteen-year-old Patrick Butler
dragged Franklin
through the streets
by the genitals.

Six white men beat,
stomped, kicked, stoned,
and hung James Costello
from a lamppost
after he shot at
and fled from
a white attacker.

Trust me, the body bags
and hashtags
from that day to this
are always in our minds,
hearts, and conversation.

It is why we are here,
sweating/smiling/
shimmying/spinning.

It is why we step
at Summit Rock
every summer.
For Seneca Village.

Sankofa. Ase.

Counterstroke

A YouTube video clip
of the Lindy Hop sequence from *Hellzapoppin'*.

A comment:
"Black Americans have given this nation, and the world so much."
I wrote, "Ase" and "Amen"
four times apiece in response.

Because nothing triggers bigots
like Black joy and prosperity,
R. Caruso tagged me:

Name 3 things blacks have given us?
Europeans have given us physics, literature, classical music,
engineering, Einstein,
Newton, Mozart, Beethoven,
Fermi, Ford,
or should I go on?
Of course I know about
jazz and the Blues.
The great black tap dancers.
I enjoy them all.
But did you think about the iPhone or Android phone you are using?
Or a computer.
Maybe an iPad.
The internet?
All invented by whites.
So accept it.

My reply:
"I don't have to accept your white supremacy.
If you are interested
in learning and reading something
other than *Mein Kampf*,

go the library or a bookstore.
Myriad books proving that throughout
human history,
Africa and the African diaspora
contributed to the advancement
of scholarship, technology, science,
architecture, medicine, literature, the arts.
Have a nice day!"

My friends in response to my Facebook post
about the incident:
You should have told him
who actually invented physics
and that cell phone he is so proud of.
You should have suggested that he read
The African Origin of Civilization
The Isis Papers
How Europe Underdeveloped Africa.

If I thought he would have cared
I would have sent the links to articles:

Imhotep and King Djoser's Step Pyramid,
hundreds of years before the Classical Age.
The Dogon, white dwarf star Sirius B,
and their naked eyes.
Beethoven's dedication of "Sonata No. 9 in A major"
to his friend and collaborator,
Black violinist George Bridgetower.

Chevalier de Saint-Georges,
who taught violin to Marie Antoinette.

Samuel Coleridge-Taylor's
*Hiawatha's Wedding Feast, African Romances,
the African Suite (1898),*
and *Toussaint l'ouverture.*

William Grant Still,
conductor, composer
of *Afro-American Symphony*.

Florence Price's *Symphony in E Minor*.
George Washington Carver
and the peanut and soil rotation.
Percy Julian's pioneering work
in synthesizing medicinal drugs from plants.
Katherine Johnson.
Gladys West and her model of the Earth for the GPS.
Walter Lincoln Hawkins's invention
of plastic coating for telephone wires,
leading to universal phone service.
Dr. Henry T. Sampson's invention
of the "Gamma-electric Cell"
led to cell phone tech.

How Einstein
supported the Scottsboro boys.
Criticized America's exploitation
and oppression of black people
in his "The Negro Question".
Invited Marian Anderson to stay at his home
when the segregated Nassau Inn of Princeton
denied her a room.
Refused to speak at universities,
except for Lincoln University,
where he called racism a disease of white people.
Worked on an anti-lynching campaign
with Paul Robeson.
Offered to be a character witness
for W.E.B. DuBois in '51
when the government indicted him
as a foreign agent.
The judge dropped the case
because of the publicity.

I took the high road with R. Caruso,
even though he and the millions like him
trigger all the ancestral anger in my DNA.

All he could do
was throw words my way.

All I had was a headache.

No
gun
noose
whip
invasion of my thighs.

Asante to the ancestors for rebelling.
Enduring.

Carla M. Cherry is a high school English teacher. Her work has appeared in various publications, including *Random Sample Review, Anti-Heroin Chic, 433, ISLE,* and *Raising Mothers.*

A Best of the Net and Pushcart Prize nominee, she authored six books of poetry: *Gnat Feathers and Butterfly Wings, Thirty Dollars and a Bowl of Soup, Honeysuckle Me, These Pearls Are Real, Stardust and Skin,* and *May He Bless My Name,* and one other chapbook, *Clap Your Hands, Stomp Your Feet* (Grandma Moses Press).

She holds an M.F.A. in Creative Writing from the City College of New York.

www.ingramcontent.com/pod-product-compliance
Lightning Source LLC
Chambersburg PA
CBHW022103080426
42734CB00009B/1468